First World War
and Army of Occupation
War Diary
France, Belgium and Germany

15 DIVISION
44 Infantry Brigade
Royal Fusiliers (City of London Regiment)
3rd Battalion
1 September 1918 - 30 September 1918

WO95/1941/4

The Naval & Military Press Ltd
www.nmarchive.com
Published in association with The National Archives

Published by

The Naval & Military Press Ltd

Unit 10 Ridgewood Industrial Park,

Uckfield, East Sussex,

TN22 5QE England

Tel: +44 (0) 1825 749494

www.naval-military-press.com

www.nmarchive.com

This diary has been reprinted in facsimile from the original. Any imperfections are inevitably reproduced and the quality may fall short of modern type and cartographic standards.

© Crown Copyright
Images reproduced by permission of The National Archives, London, England, 2015.

Contents

Document type	Place/Title	Date From	Date To
Heading	3 Bttn Royal Fusiliers Sep 1918 1941 1941/4		
Miscellaneous	Vol 4 War Diary 3rd Battalion Royal Fusiliers September 1918. (One Appendix attached)		
War Diary	Martin Eglise Camp No 4	01/09/1918	15/09/1918
War Diary	Battn Hdqrs. Chateau Ivergny.	15/09/1918	26/09/1918
War Diary	Battn Hdqrs Contay. High St.	27/09/1918	28/09/1918
War Diary	Battn. Hdqes. Nurlu Sheet 62 c 1/40000 Go-ad D 4 & 6.6.	29/09/1918	30/09/1918
Operation(al) Order(s)	3rd. Battalion Royal Fusiliers. Operation Order No. 1	15/09/1918	15/09/1918

5 1941
1941/4 3 Bttn Royal
Fusiliers

Sep 1918

149/50

45-C. (8 sheets)

Army Form A. 2007.

CENTRAL REGISTRY.

Central Registry No. and Date.

Attached Files.

SUBJECT, AND OFFICE OF ORIGIN.

War Diary

3rd Battalion Royal Fusiliers

September 1918.

(one appendix attached)

Army Form C. 2118.

WAR DIARY
or
INTELLIGENCE SUMMARY.
(Erase heading not required.)

3rd Battalion Royal Fusiliers

Instructions regarding War Diaries and Intelligence Summaries are contained in F.S. Regs., Part II. and the Staff Manual respectively. Title pages will be prepared in manuscript.

Place	Date	Hour	Summary of Events and Information	Remarks and references to Appendices
MARTIN EGLISE, Camp No 4.	September 1918		Battalion in duty:-	
	1st.		Capt J.M. McLAGGAN. M.C. regained from leave in U.K. + resumed duties of Regimental Medical Officer. Capt R.T.C. CHADWICK. do do + took over command of No 4 Coy from LIEUT D.S. CORLETT.	
	2nd.		Company Training. Section & artillery officer of 50th Divn Artillery on recent fighting to all officers + N.C.O's	
			Went on duty at 5.30 p.m. in camp theatre	
			LIEUT B J O'CONNOR regained from leave in U.K.	
			" R A L DAVIES. do do	
			Capts+Capt. W T HUMPHREYS. do do 149 Bde Hdqrs on ceasing to be attached reassumed duties of adjutant. VICE Lieut S A TURNER lewis gun officer.	
	3rd.		Company Training. a demonstration of Smoke Barrage was given Bg149 + T.M.B. to the Battalion	
		150 Brig	Bombing Grounds. also of message carrying Rockets. at 2.30 p.m.	
			CAPT R.D.T WOOLFE. regained from leave in U.K.	
			CAPT. C.H. BAILMACHE. do do do .	
			LIEUT. A.S. BALDING. do do do .	
	4th.		Divisional Route March. Whole Battalion a transport - duss fighting order. distance 14 miles. Route. ANCOURT - BELLENGREVILLE - ENVERMU - ST NICOLAS - ARCHELLES - MARTIN EGLISE - No of men falling out = NIL. Battalion on Duty.	REF. MAP DIEPPE SHEET No 16 1/100,000.
			2/LT I T MORRIS. rejoined from leave in U.K.	

Army Form C. 2118.

WAR DIARY
or
INTELLIGENCE SUMMARY.
(Erase heading not required.)

8th Battn Royal Fusiliers

Place	Date	Hour	Summary of Events and Information	Remarks and references to Appendices
MARTIN EGLISE Camp No 4.	September 1918 5th		DIVISIONAL TACTICAL EXERCISE to be held on the 6th inst. 149 Bde to represent the enemy holding a defensive line BERNEVAL - GRAINCOURT - 32A Battn Royal Fusiliers, in Brigade Reserve in MARTIN-EN-CAMPAGNE. Battalion paraded as strong as possible with transport Reconnoitering at 4 pm marched in ANCOURT - GRAINCOURT - ST MARTIN-EN-CAMPAGNE - where it billetted for the night 5/6 inst in the village of ST MARTIN-EN-CAMPAGNE.	Ref Staff DIEPPE 1/100000 Sheet 16.
	6th		Battalion stood to in defensive position at 5.30 a.m. attacked by 1504 151 Bdes. Withdrew line by 8.30 a.m. Operations ceased at 9.15 a.m. Battalion Reinforced marched back to Camp by some route as 5th inst arriving in camp 1 p.m. 2nd Lt. G. R. E. H. NICHOLSON D.S.O. rejoined from leave in U.K. & took over Command of the Battalion from Major W. A. TRASENSTER M.C. LIEUT. W. E. FORSTER. rejoined from leave in U.K.	
	7th		Battalion on Duty: Working parties detailed under Brigade Orders - Company Training	
	8th		Voluntary Church Service. Lecture to officers and NCO's at 5.0 p.m. in Camp theatre by Commander G. B. SPICER-SIMSON, D.S.O. Naval Staff. Intelligence dinner on "The Anti-Submarine Campaign."	
	9th		(a) The function of the fleet. (A) The Bangs. Bombing. Grenade Company Training. 30 yds Bangs. 300 yds Bangs, Assault course. Lectures Formations. 600 yds Bangs.	

Army Form C. 2118.

WAR DIARY
or
INTELLIGENCE SUMMARY.

(Erase heading not required.)

3rd Battalion Royal Fusiliers

Instructions regarding War Diaries and Intelligence Summaries are contained in F.S. Regs., Part II. and the Staff Manual respectively. Title pages will be prepared in manuscript.

Place	Date	Hour	Summary of Events and Information	Remarks and references to Appendices
MARTIN EGLISE Camp No.4.	September 1916 9th		(continued). The following Lectures were given at 10 a.m. "Bayonet Fighting" by Lieut. CP. CAMPBELL D.S.O. & at 11.45 a.m. to officers + N.C.O.S. on "Amiens-the War" by Dr. A. IRVINE.	
	10th		Major W.A TRASENSTER M.O. proceeded on leave to U.K.	
			Battalion on Duty. Working parties under Brigade Orders. Remainder in Company training with	
	11th		2/LT. H.B. LEAVERS struck the Battalion from 6th Battn. U.K. on posting. seven guns given a total	
			Company Training. 300-300 Range about courses. Bombing practice on ground	
			Divisional Tactical exercise, attack in neighbourhood of ST.MARTIN-EN-CAMPAGNE & PENLY. R/F MAP PIEPPE Sheet No 16.	
	12th		operations commenced 10 a.m. & ceased 1.15 p.m. division out - marched out about 6 p.m. the whole Battalion including its own transport & ammunition took part in this exercise.	
	13th		Battn. on duty. shooting on 300yds SMLE	
			Company training.	
	14th		Divisional Platoon shooting competition, at Brigade butts, 300yds Range.	
	15th		2/LT. H.MARSH rejoined from Cadre, U.K. 2/LT. L. BROWNHURST admitted Hospital.	
			Orders received for move to next area. Battalion entrained at 7. P.M. at ARQUES LA BATAILLE station operation now attached.	
Batt. HeadQrs. CHATEAU, IVERGNY	16th		for BOUQUESMAISON complete with transport. Strength 36. officers + 649 other ranks.	
			Camp at BOUQUESMAISON Station at 7 a.m. + marched to the village of IVERGNY where the Battalion REF MAP LENS Sheet 11. 1/100,000	
			was billeted. breakfast on arrival. at 8 a.m. Cleaning billets the remainder of day - until	
	17th		Battalion tactical exercises (the attack) between IVERGNY + SUS ST. LEGER. Companies on 30yds	
	18th		Range in afternoon. Battalion issued with 16 Lewis Guns, completing the Battalion to 36 Guns.	
			Battalion tactical exercises as on 17th inst.	

WAR DIARY
or
INTELLIGENCE SUMMARY.

(Erase heading not required.)

Army Form C. 2118.

3rd Battalion Royal Fusiliers

Place	Date	Hour	Summary of Events and Information	Remarks and references to Appendices
Batt. Hqrs. CHATEAU IVERGNY.	September 19th 1918		Brigade tactical exercise on ground N.W. of IVERGNY towards REBREUVIETTE (the attack). Battalion parade 9.15 a.m. dismissed on return to camp. Dress Fighting order.	REF MAP LENS Sheet 11 1/10000
	20th inst		Battalion Route March. Dress Fighting order, starting pt. cross Roads W. of IVERGNY Church at 10 a.m. Route ROSIERE - REBREUVIETTE - MON LEBLOND - ROQUES MAISON - LE SOUICH - IVERGNY. Dinners at MON LEBLOND. Battalion returned to camp 5 PM C.O. expressed his appreciation of splendid Marching of the Men. Battalion not state - NIL - Weather INCLEMENT. Strength + 30 other ranks. LIEUT F PARKER. returned from leave in U.K.	
	21st		Brigade tactical exercise on 20th 19th inst. Section 3.30 PM for all Officers.	
	22nd		Sunday - Voluntary Church parade 9.30 a.m. "Battalion N.C.O.s on "Co-operation between Tanks + Infantry" by Lt. Col. MCKELHAM D.S.O. Demonstration of platoon in attack and range firing ass.	
	23rd			
	24th		Battalion Route March. Dress Fighting order, starting point cross roads E of IVERGNY CHURCH at 8.30 a.m. Route BEAUDRICOURT - ETREE - WAMIN - HENVAL - FREVENT - BONNIERES - CANTLEAUX - NEUVILLETTE - BOUQUEMAISON - LE SOUICH - IVERGNY. Battalion returned to camp at 6.30 PM. distance 18 miles. Falling out state NIL - Weather fine - MARCHING excellent.	

Army Form C. 2118.

WAR DIARY
or
INTELLIGENCE SUMMARY.
(Erase heading not required.)

3rd Battalion Bedfordshire

Place	Date	Hour	Summary of Events and Information	Remarks and references to Appendices
Batt. Hdqrs. Chateau IVERGNY.	September 25th 1918.		Company training under company arrangements. etc.	
	26		Battalion orders to move - entrained at 8.30 a.m. for CONTAY - train 5.15 - 5.7 - LEBERGY. LUCHEUX, DOULLENS, VILLERS BOCAGE - BEHENCOURT - arrived 4 PM & went into Billets.	L&V's Sheet 11. Hbrag.
Batt. Hdqrs. CONTAY. High St.	27		at CONTAY. MAJOR W.A.TRASENSTER M.C. rejoined from leave in U.K.	57.C S.E. 6 N.W. Sheet
	28		Battalion orders to move - to NORLU. - Entrained at 1 P.M. train via ALBERT - FRICOURT. Battalion arrived de-bussed at 7.30. P.M. and marched to NORLU. arriving at 10.30 P.M. went into Billets	57 C 1/20000 Sh 57 C AMIENS sheet 62 c/20000 City sheet 1/20000 57. C. 1/40000
Batt. Hdqrs. NORLU Huts B2C lborrow	29		at NORLU. arrangements for trenches at 1 hours notice - stood by all day - 7 P.M. orders received. Rest night.	
NORLU. Huts B2C lborrow Go-od D4 & b.b.	30		at NORLU arrangements for trenches at 1 hours notice 1st October with was told harness 1st October with	57 C. 1/40000

Fighting strength on 30/9/18. 36 officers and 686 other ranks. (includes 13 officers and 137 other ranks in battle surplus)

Evacuated sick with malaria 16
Other causes 12

A.G. Spalding Lieut
9/x/18 3/R. Beds

D D. & I. London, E.C.
A co) Wt. W. 71/M2031 750,000 5/17 Sch. 52 Forms C2. 0/14

3rd. Battalion Royal Fusiliers.

SECRET.

OPERATION ORDER No.1.

Ref. Map.
DIEPPE 1/100,000.

In the Field,
15th Sept.1918.

1. MOVE. The 149th Infantry Brigade will move to new area to-day, entraining at ARQUES LA BATAILLE Station at 6.p.m.

2. PARADE. The Battalion will parade at 5.p.m. formed up in close column of Companies in following order:-
Bn.H.Q. No.s 1,2,3 and 4 Coys.

3. DRESS. Full marching order. Blankets will be carried in the pack. and greatcoats over the arm.

4. Baggage.etc. All baggage, stores, equipment, officers kits and officers mess to be loaded at 2.p.m.

5. TRANSPORT. The R.T.O. will arrange to send all transport to Qr.Mrs. Stores by 12 noon and will move at 3.p.m.

6. RETURNS. Marching out states will be forwarded to this office by 12 noon.

7. DETAILS. Lieut. J. Hart and all details remaining behind will move to No.1.Camp to-morrow.

Issued at 11.15.a.m.

Captain.

Adjutant 3rd. Battalion Royal Fusiliers.

Copies to:-

All Coys., Bn.H.Q., Qr.Mr., R.T.O. Retained and War Diary.